Hazardous Materials Management/
Abandoned Mine Land Management

Applicable or Relevant and Appropriate Requirements

Determining Which Federal and State Regulations
Apply in the Cleanup Process

TR-1703-1/TR-3720-1

BY:

Pamela S. Innis

Bureau of Land Management

National Science and Technology Center

Denver, Colorado

United States Department of the Interior
Bureau of Land Management

Suggested Citation

Innis, Pamela S. 2007. Applicable or relevant and appropriate requirements: Determining which federal and state regulations apply in the cleanup process. Technical Reference 1703-1/3720-1. Bureau of Land Management, Denver, Colorado. BLM/ST/ST-07/006+1703+3720. 39 pages.

As the lead Federal agency for actions taken on public lands administered by the Bureau of Land Management, the BLM is responsible for the identification of all environmental laws that pertain to the investigation and clean up of abandoned mines and other contaminated sites. This technical reference provides information to BLM abandoned mine land (AML) and hazardous materials site managers on how they may determine which Federal and State regulations apply to their cleanup activities. Examples and case studies are given for further insight into this process.

Abstract

Under the authority of the Comprehensive Environmental Response, Compensation, and Liability Act (CERCLA or Superfund) of 1980, as amended, and pursuant to the National Oil and Hazardous Substances Pollution Contingency Plan (NCP), the Department of the Interior has been delegated the responsibility for undertaking response actions with respect to the release or threat of release of oil, petroleum products, hazardous substances, or pollutants and contaminants, that pose an actual or potential threat to human health or welfare, or to the environment. Under this authority, the Bureau of Land Management (BLM) may take an action to protect public land resources and public land users from hazardous substances that pose a threat or potential threat to human health and the environment. As the lead Federal agency for actions taken on public land administered by the BLM, the Bureau is responsible for the identification of all environmental laws that pertain to any CERCLA cleanup actions.

Neither CERCLA nor the NCP contain cleanup levels or performance standards for use in evaluating and selecting actions. The Environmental Protection Agency (EPA) did, however, specify in the NCP that actions taken under CERCLA would attain applicable or relevant and appropriate Federal standards (ARARs) in CERCLA response actions. In the 1986 revision of CERCLA (the Superfund Amendment and Reauthorization Act or SARA), Congress codified the existing approach to compliance with other laws. CERCLA Section 121(d)(2)(A)(ii) specifies that on-site actions must attain Federal standards, requirements, criteria, limitations, or more stringent State standards determined to be legally applicable or relevant and appropriate to the circumstances at a given site.

Applicable requirements are cleanup standards, standards of control, and other substantive requirements, criteria or limitations promulgated under Federal environmental or State environmental or facility siting laws that directly and fully address a hazardous substance, pollutant, contaminant, action being taken, location, or other circumstances found at a CERCLA site.

Applicability is a legal and jurisdictional determination, while relevance and appropriateness relies on the professional judgement of the individual performing the analysis utilizing information pertinent to the specific site.

> **Example:** Closure requirements under Subtitle C of RCRA are applicable at a landfill that received RCRA hazardous waste after 1980 or where the action constitutes disposal of hazardous waste. In this case, the site must be closed in compliance with one of the closure options available in Subtitle C regulations.

Relevant and appropriate requirements are cleanup standards, standards of control, and other substantive requirements, criteria, or limitations promulgated under Federal environmental or State environmental or facility siting laws that, while not "applicable" to a hazardous substance, pollutant, contaminant, action, location, or other circumstances at the CERCLA site, address similar problems or situations to those encountered at the site. A requirement that is relevant and appropriate may not meet one or more of the jurisdictional prerequisites for applicability, but it still may make sense to apply it at the site, given the circumstances of the site and nature of the release.

Once a requirement is determined to be relevant and appropriate, it must be complied with as if it were applicable. Whether or not a requirement is relevant and appropriate will vary depending on factors such as the duration of the response action, the form or concentration of the contaminants present, the nature of the release, the availability of other standards that more directly match the circumstances at the site, and other factors specified in the Code of Federal Regulations at 40 CFR 300.400(g)(2)) and identified in Table 1.

Table 1. Factors to Determine Whether Requirements are Relevant and Appropriate.

40CFR§300.400 (g)(2) If, based upon paragraph (g)(1) of this section, it is determined that a requirement is not applicable to a specific release, the requirement may still be relevant and appropriate to the circumstances of the release. In evaluating relevance and appropriateness, the factors in paragraphs (g)(2)(i) through (viii) of this section shall be examined, where pertinent, to determine whether a requirement addresses problems or situations sufficiently similar to the circumstances of the release or remedial action contemplated, and whether the requirement is well-suited to the site, and therefore is both relevant and appropriate. The pertinence of each of the following factors will depend, in part, on whether a requirement addresses a chemical, location, or action. The following comparisons shall be made, where pertinent, to determine relevance and appropriateness:

(i) The purpose of the requirement and the purpose of the CERCLA action;

(ii) The medium regulated or affected by the requirement and the medium contaminated or affected at the CERCLA site;

(iii) The substances regulated by the requirement and the substances found at the CERCLA site;

(iv) The actions or activities regulated by the requirement and the remedial action contemplated at the CERCLA site;

(v) Any variances, waivers, or exemptions of the requirement and their availability for the circumstances at the CERCLA site;

(vi) The type of place regulated and the type of place affected by the release or CERCLA action;

(vii) The type and size of structure or facility regulated and the type and size of structure or facility affected by the release or contemplated by the CERCLA action;

(viii) Any consideration of use or potential use of affected resources in the requirement and the use or potential use of the affected resource at the CERCLA site.

An overly broad interpretation of the "relevant and appropriate" concept may result in a number of requirements needing waivers, where a more defined and refined analysis may eliminate many of the potential requirements as, although relevant, not appropriate to the specifics of the situation.

Example: The Bevill exclusion (RCRA 3001(b)(3)(A)(ii)) excludes "solid waste from the extraction, beneficiation and processing of ores and minerals" from regulation as hazardous waste under Subtitle C of RCRA. However, under certain situations where the mine waste may be considered high risk due to concentration of contaminants, the site manager may make the determination to consider Subtitle C closure requirements as relevant and appropriate. In this case, a "hybrid closure," which includes other types of closure designs, may be used.

Applicable or relevant and appropriate requirements should be identified early on in the cleanup process during the site evaluation. Site managers should consider potential chemical specific standards for their project during the preliminary assessment. Site characterization data must be compared to background concentrations and appropriate cleanup standards, therefore detection limits of analytical procedures must achieve these standards.

During removal actions, ARARs are identified when practicable depending upon site circumstances, and attainment of ARARs is dependent on the exigency of the situation and the scope of the removal action. An ARAR analysis is found in an Engineering Evaluation/Cost Analysis (EE/CA) for a non-time-critical removal action. During the streamlined risk assessment, contaminant concentrations can be compared to chemical-specific ARARs to identify the need for an action. ARARs are also used in the evaluation of removal alternatives.

During a Remedial Investigation/Feasibility Study (RI/FS) process, chemical- and location-specific ARARs are identified as part of the characterization activities for the site. ARARs must be identified relative to the characteristics of the particular site and the substances at the site. The BLM should provide information concerning contaminant types and affected media to assist the State in identification of ARARs. During the FS, action-specific ARARs, relative to cleanup alternatives selected to address the particular circumstances at the site, are introduced. All ARARs are used in the evaluation of alternatives.

The process of identifying ARARs for removal or remedial actions begins with initial site characterization and continues through the design phase. In completing an ARAR analysis, the requirements are typically presented in the document in four basic groups:

- Chemical-specific standards established for specific chemicals found on the site
- Location-specific restrictions based on the location of the site
- Action-specific limitations on "actions" associated with a response
- Other information To Be Considered (TBC)

Chemical-specific requirements are usually health, risk, or technology based standards that limit the concentration of a chemical (such as a metal) or chemical compound (such as a pesticide) at a site. Chemical-specific ARARs generally set human or environmental risk-based criteria and protocol which, when applied to site-specific conditions, result in the establishment of numerical action values. These values establish the acceptable amount or concentration of a chemical that may be found in, or discharged to, the ambient environment.

> **Example:** National Primary and Secondary Drinking Water Standards, 40 CFR 141 and 143. A list of Federal ARARs to consider that are chemical-specific may be found in the Appendix, Table A-1.

Location-specific requirements relate to the geographic or physical position of the site, rather than to the nature of site contaminants. These ARARs place restrictions on the concentration of hazardous substances or the conduct of cleanup activities due to their location in the environment.

> **Example:** Native American Graves Protection and Repatriation Act, 25 USC 3001–3013 and 43 CFR 10. A list of Federal ARARs to consider that are location-specific may be found in the Appendix, Table A-2.

Action-specific requirements are usually technology- or activity-based requirements or are limitations on actions taken with respect to hazardous substances. A particular activity will trigger action-specific ARARs. Unlike chemical-specific and location-specific ARARs, action-specific ARARs do not, in themselves, determine the alternative. Rather, action-specific ARARs indicate how the selected cleanup alternative should be implemented.

> **Example:** Hazardous Materials Transportation Act, 49 USC 1801–1813 and 40 CFR 107, 171–177. A list of Federal ARARs to consider that are action-specific may be found in the Appendix, Table A-3.

Non-promulgated advisories or guidance documents issued by Federal or State governments do not have the status of potential ARARs. However, these advisories and guidance are "to be considered" (TBC) when determining protective cleanup levels, as defined in 40 CFR 300.400 (g)(3). TBCs generally fall within three categories: health effects information with a high degree of credibility; technical information on how to perform or evaluate site investigations or response actions; and agency policy or guidance.

> **Example:** BLM Technical Note 390 – Risk Management Criteria for Metals at BLM Mining Sites. A list of TBCs to consider that are location-specific may be found in the Appendix, Table A-4.

Many States implement environmental regulations that differ from Federal standards. CERCLA Section 121(d)(2)(ii) requires compliance with applicable or relevant and appropriate State requirements when they are more stringent than Federal rules and have been "promulgated" at the State level. To be viewed as promulgated and serve as ARARs at a CERCLA site, a State requirement must be legally enforceable, based on specific enforcement provisions or the State's general legal authority, and must be generally applicable, meaning that it applies to a broader universe than just CERCLA sites. Requirements that are developed by a local or regional body and are both promulgated and legally enforceable by the State may, however, also serve as ARARs.

Examples of environmental standards that are often more stringent at the State level and that function as State ARARs include hazardous waste facility siting restrictions under the Resource Conservation and Recovery Act (RCRA), Clean Water Act (CWA) toxic pollutant discharge limits, and CWA anti-degradation requirements for surface water and ground water.

> **Example:** Total Maximum Daily Load (TMDL) Regulation. TMDLs may be established by the EPA or by the individual States and tribes, depending on who has authority to administer the Clean Water Act (CWA) in a particular area. TMDLs established by the States and tribes must be approved by the EPA. Point-source pollution allocations have been established in TMDLs through the use of National Pollution Elimination Discharge (NPDES) permits. TMDLs for non-point source pollution allocations are not promulgated as rules, are not enforceable, and are therefore not ARARs. These TMDLs may be considered a TBC.

The statutory waivers in CERCLA Section 121(d)(4) apply when considering State ARARs as well. State ARARs do not have to be attained where the standard, requirement, criterion, or limitation has not been consistently applied in circumstance similar to the response in question.

CERCLA Section 121 (e) provides that "no Federal, State, or local permit shall be required for the portion of any removal or remedial action conducted entirely on site, when the action is in compliance with cleanup standards" Only the substantive elements of other laws affect on-site responses. This permit exemption allows the response action to proceed in an expeditious manner, free from potentially lengthy delays associated with the permit process. The lack of permitting authority does not impede implementation of an environmentally protective remedy, since CERCLA and the NCP already provide a procedural blueprint for responding to the release or threatened release of a hazardous substance into the environment.

CERCLA Section 121(d)(4) provides a listing of the circumstances where ARARs can be waived as long as the remedy is protective of human health and the environment. The six waivers follow.

Interim Action

CERCLA Section 121(d)(4)(A) specifies that a waiver may be considered if the action selected is only part of a total remedial action that will attain such level or standard of control when completed. These waivers may be used for situations when:

- Temporary measures are part of the final action
- Final action must achieve ARAR compliance within a reasonable period of time
- Interim measure may not cause or worsen problems at the site or hinder the final remedy

   Example: Water running over a tailings site during a storm picks up contaminants and washes them into a nearby river. The site is capped as an interim measure to prevent further contamination of the river. The current location of the tailings is not preferred for a repository, therefore the cap does not achieve final remediation of the contaminated material or cleanup of the river to State water quality standards.

Greater Risk to Health and the Environment

CERCLA Section 121(d)(4)(B) specifies that a waiver may be considered if compliance with such requirement at the site will result in greater risk to human health and the environment than alternative options or noncompliance. Considerations for this type of waiver include the:

- Magnitude of adverse impacts
- Risk posed by remedy using waiver
- Duration of adverse impacts
- Reversibility of adverse impacts

Example: Metal laden sediment coming from an old mine tailings site is found in river sediment. Although the tailings have been cleaned up, the metal concentrations exceed sediment criteria. However, the sediment is overlain by clean sediment from natural erosion. Dredging the river bottom to obtain the metals-contaminated sediment would result in a release of the metals to the river waters and endanger aquatic life and human health. No risk to humans or aquatic life would result from leaving the sediments in place.

Technical Impracticability

CERCLA Section 121(d)(4)(C) specifies that a waiver may be considered if compliance with such requirement is technically impracticable from an engineering perspective. The waiver may not be invoked merely because compliance would require implementation of innovative or alternative technologies. The primary factors to be considered are:

- Engineering Feasibility. Compliance with an ARAR is considered infeasible from an engineering perspective if current engineering methods necessary to construct and maintain an alternative that is ARAR compliant cannot be reasonably implemented.
- Reliability. The term "impracticability" is based on the balance of engineering feasibility and reliability. The reliability is based on whether or not the remedy

can be relied upon to attain the ARAR. This waiver is most often used for final groundwater remedies that cannot achieve MCLs because of site-specific hydrogeologic and contaminant conditions.

- Cost. This applies only if the cost of compliance is highly excessive.

Examples:

Cherokee County Site, Cherokee County, Kansas – 1997, 1989: Technical Impracticability Waivers were granted for two of six different subsites in this former mining area. The first waiver was applied to the Galena subsite for acid mine drainage in the shallow groundwater. The second waiver was applied to the Baxter Springs and Treece subsites (18,000 acres collectively), due to the fact that compliance would be "inordinately costly" ($93 million in 1994 dollars). The Cherokee County site is part of the Tri-State Mining District, which was mined for approximately 100 years.

Summitville Mine, Rio Grande County, Colorado – 2001: Cyanide, acid, and metal-laden water flows into the Alamosa River. Remediation actions are currently underway, under the direction of the State of Colorado. State surface water standards have been waived for pH, aluminium, iron, and aquatic life, due to the presence of naturally occurring minerals that contribute metals and acidity.

Equivalent Standard of Performance

CERCLA Section 121(d)(4)(D) specifies that a waiver may be considered if the action selected will attain a standard of performance that is equivalent to that required under the otherwise applicable standard, requirement, criteria, or limitation, through use of another method or approach. Considerations for utilizing this type of waiver include:

- Time requirements of proposed action compared to time requirements of alternative that achieves compliance
- Degree to which proposed action protects human health and the environment
- Level of performance of proposed action
- Future reliability of proposed action

> **Example:** RCRA hazardous wastes may be disposed of on land if they meet the Best Demonstrated Available Technology (BDAT) set by EPA for that hazardous waste. If a newly-developed or alternate technology can be shown to achieve the same cleanup levels as the BDAT, it would be considered an equivalent standard of performance.

Inconsistent Application of State Standard

CERCLA Section 121(d)(4)(E) specifies that a waiver may be considered with respect to a State standard, requirement, criteria, or limitation, if the State has not consistently applied (or demonstrated the intention to consistently apply) the standard, requirement, criteria, or limitation in similar circumstances at other sites. Considerations for this type of waiver include:

- Similarity of site or circumstances
- Proportion of noncompliance cases
- Reason for non-compliance
- Intention to consistently apply future requirements

Additionally, under CERCLA Section 120(a)(4), State laws are excluded if they apply more stringent standards and requirements to a Federal facility/site than the standards and requirements applied to facilities not owned by the Federal Government.

> **Example:** A mine drainage treatment system is installed at a site. The State demands cleanup of the water to background concentrations for this system. Further investigation shows that the cleanup levels are Federal maximum contaminant levels (MCLs) at a similar site in the same watershed. This is an inconsistent application of the standard.

Fund Balancing

This waiver applies to Superfund sites and is not available to BLM.

BLM site managers have the lead for determining whether ARARs should be waived for removal and remedial actions. It is important to discuss potentially applicable ARAR waivers with contractors and Federal and State agencies when they are recognized. All documents that identify ARARs should also discuss potential waivers that may be invoked. Those documents include the EE/CA, RI report, FS report, and proposed plan. ARAR waivers are formally documented in action memorandum for removal actions or in the record of decision (ROD).

Although the NCP explains the criteria for justifying a waiver, it does not specifically address how to waive the requirement. This should be coordinated with the regulators on a site-specific basis. It should be noted that the EPA has approval authority for the remedy selection at National Priorities List (NPL) sites, and therefore, at such sites, the EPA has the power to effectively approve or disapprove all ARAR waivers.

For more information on ARARs, visit the EPA Superfund website at *http://www. epa.gov/superfund/action/guidance/remedy/arars.htm.*

For information on ARAR waivers, visit the EPA Superfund website at *http://www.epa.gov/superfund/action/guidance/remedy/arars/waivers.htm.*

Additional Information

Hazardous Waste or Not?

Rather than a single case study, this section summarizes several sites concerning the regulatory status of the waste, which can affect permissible disposal alternatives and cost. In most States, overburden and mine waste from the extraction and beneficiation of ore is RCRA exempt. Beneficiation means processing, especially crushing, so waste rock dumps and mine tailings are not classified as hazardous waste under RCRA regardless of whether they fail the toxicity characteristic leaching procedure (TCLP). This exemption makes it easier and less expensive to manage mine waste from most AML sites. In those States, the TCLP test is not recommended for site characterization. However, California and Washington are exceptions. California uses a waste extraction test (WET), which is similar to the TCLP and Washington uses the TCLP.

- At the Davis Mine in California, the BLM tested mine tailings (RCRA exempt) using the WET test and found none of the metals of concern failed the test, hence the waste was classified as non-hazardous and could be either disposed of on site in a repository or could be sent to a solid waste landfill. Had the waste failed the test, it could still be disposed in an on site repository or be sent to a more costly and more distant hazardous waste landfill. An example of that case was the Rinconada Mine also in California. Here the waste passed the TCLP for mercury, but failed the WET test, so the waste was shipped to a hazardous waste landfill for treatment and disposal.

- At the Red Devil mine in Alaska, some of the contaminated soil had percentage concentrations of mercury that were from retorting not beneficiation. Wastes designated hazardous under Federal regulations must be treated to a certain concentration before they can be disposed of in a hazardous waste landfill. In the case of mercury from Red Devil, wastes >260 mg/kg were required to be retorted or roasted for costly treatment and still meet treatment standards. In the case of Rinconada Mine wastes, <260 mg/kg were treated (normally stabilized with Portland cement or similar reagent) to reduce the TCLP prior to being disposed of in a hazardous waste landfill.

- In a final example, at the Arrastra Dump in Colorado, trash and other solid waste was contaminated with metals, especially lead. Some soil and paper reagent bags failed the TCLP. Since this was not an obvious beneficiation waste, the material failing TCLP was designated hazardous waste and will be sent to a hazardous waste landfill where it will be treated prior to disposal. The rest of the solid waste will be sent to a solid waste landfill.

Repository – Anvil Points Facility, Rifle, Colorado

Anvil Points Repository Location

The State of Colorado conducted studies of the waste shale pile at the Anvil Points facility and concluded that several inorganic elements were leaching (or eroding) into surface water from the pile, but only iron appeared to be at concentrations exceeding Colorado Water Quality Standards. Aluminum, arsenic, boron, barium, chromium, cobalt, copper, iron, lithium, magnesium, manganese, molybdenum, sodium, nickel, lead, vanadium, and zinc are present in the spent shale in concentrations that are significantly above background soil concentrations. Arsenic is the only inorganic in the waste shale pile that exceeds constituent specific residential (unrestrictive) risk based standards.

The selected alternative for cleanup of spent (retorted) shale and raw shale fines (excluded from the retorting process) was excavation and placement of the waste shale into an on-site repository (see photo). Samples were taken to characterize the waste and the TCLP analysis was performed. The results indicated that the waste was not considered a hazardous waste.

An ARARs analysis was completed and it was determined that the constructed on-site repository must comply with Federal and Colorado solid waste regulations. The specific regulations applied to the repository are the Colorado Solid Wastes Disposal Sites and Facilities Act and subsequent Regulations: CRS Title 30, Article 20, Part 1 as amended and 6 CCR 1007-2, Part 1 – Regulations Pertaining to Solid Waste Sites and Facilities, Sections 1, 2 and 3; and, to a lesser extent, the Federal Criteria for Municipal Solid Waste Landfills, 40 CFR Part 258.

Repository – Anvil Points Facility, Rifle, Colorado, and Poorman/Balm Creek, Baker City, Oregon

Poorman/Balm Creek

The waste rock and tailings generated during the operation of the mine are not considered a "hazardous waste" as defined by RCRA 40 CFR 261. Under 40 CFR 261.4(b)(7), the Bevill Exclusion, solid waste from the extraction and beneficiation of ores and minerals are excluded from the definition of hazardous waste and therefore are not subject to RCRA Subtitle C requirements.

Although not considered a hazardous waste, the two tailings dams are in the flood plain and a significant flood event would be expected to breach one or both of the dams, releasing tailings in a mudflow down gradient. While there are no human receptors in the immediate path, such a release would multiply the costs of cleanup and present an immediate, significant risk to aquatic life, particularly trout. Expeditious containment of the tailings will eliminate risks from direct contact to humans and wildlife and will reduce release of metals to the Balm Creek downstream.

The selected alternative for disposal of tailings was removal and transportation and disposal in an on-site repository. The repository area is located west of the Balm Creek Mine site and away from Balm Creek. The Oregon regulation governing "Solid Waste: Land Disposal Sites other than MSW Landfills," Oregon Administrative Rules, OAR Chapter 340 Division 95, regulates the siting, operation, and maintenance of any non-municipal land disposal site. Specifically, it was determined that the siting, operation and maintenance of the repository shall, to the extent practicable, comply with the criteria specified in OAR 340-095-0010 Location Restrictions; 340-095-0020, 6 through 8, Operating Criteria specific to surface water and endangered species; 340-095-0030 Design Criteria; and 340-095-0040 Groundwater Monitoring and Corrective Action.

The BLM provided documentation for justification of a waiver of the OAR Chapter 340 Division 95(0070)(2)(a), which requires 3 feet of cover material. The alternative design specifies two feet of cover material, and the design is based on the type of waste, climate, geological setting, and the degree of environmental impact. The Oregon Department of Environmental Quality (ODEQ) agreed to BLM's waiver for OAR 340 Division 95(0070)(2)(a) in correspondence dated October 26, 2004, which provided comments on the design documents. ODEQ stated that "the design, including the alternative cover proposed for the tailings and waste rock repository, is very detailed and appears to be protective of human health and the environment" and that "The Department has no further comments on the proposed design."

Run-on/run-off controls are established along the outer edge of the repository. The cap will be graded to promote drainage and vegetated with native grasses and forbes. A monitoring well was installed down-gradient of the repository to address potential impacts to groundwater. The well was constructed in accordance with Well Construction Standards, OAR Chapter 690 Division 240.

Water Quality Criteria – Old Granby Landfill, Grand County, Colorado

The Granby Landfill is located in Grand County, Colorado, approximately 3 miles northwest of the town of Granby. The ephemeral Coyote Creek is 100 yards to the west of the landfill and flows south to the Colorado River, which is located less than ¼ mile away. Two small ephemeral drainages cross the site with an approximate north-northeast to southwesterly orientation and join below the landfill. The northernmost of these two drainages is fed by a large spring complex located immediately to the north of the landfill. A very small spring emanates from the middle landfill cell and flows a short distance into the smaller ephemeral drainage. The landfill was a Recreational and Public Purpose (R&PP) lease beginning in 1961 and was placed on the EPA's Federal Facility Docket after the landfill closed in 1976. CERCLA investigations ended after completion of an Expanded Remedial Site Inspection (RSI), which sampled three groundwater monitoring wells and five surface water and sediment stations over a 6-year period.

Based upon site characterization results the potential exposure pathways were found to be through the surface water and/or groundwater. Therefore, the ARAR analysis focused on these media. Two documents governing surface water quality standards in Colorado were reviewed to assess potential impacts from the landfill. The Colorado Water Quality Control Commission (WQCC) provides basic regulations found in Colorado Department of Public Health and the Environment (CDPHE) WQCC's Regulation No.31 – The Basic Standards and Methodologies for Surface Water. Because various watersheds within Colorado require explicit protection, the location of the site and its watershed dictate which classifications and numeric standards may also apply. For the Granby Landfill area, this regulation is WQCC's Regulation 33 - Classifications and Numeric Standards for Upper Colorado River Basin and North Platte River (Region 12). Segment 6a of this listing for the Granby Landfill area is designated as Aquatic Life Cold Water 1, Recreation 2, Water Supply and Agriculture. It specifically identifies standards for dissolved oxygen, pH, fecal coliform, ammonia, residual chlorine, chloride, sulfide, sulfate, nitrate, nitrite, arsenic, boron, cadmium, trivalent and hexavalent chromium, copper, iron, lead, manganese, mercury, nickel, selenium, silver and zinc, while referring to Regulation No. 31 for organic standards.

In addition, standards regulating the quality of groundwater were also reviewed. Although the EPA's Maximum Contaminant Levels (MCLs) are applicable, the CDPHE's Regulation 41 – Basic Standards for Groundwater and Regulation 42 Site Specific Classifications also apply and their requirements are generally lower than those of the MCLs. In addition, these regulations provide a division of the standards based upon groundwater use, for example, domestic use and agricultural use.

Although several releases to surface water were found emanating from an on-site spring, the thorough RSI characterization information provided the evidence to eliminate these as surface water releases by understanding the seasonality of an ephemeral system. Specifically, during seasonal high-flow, no releases were detected, and during low-flow, no surface water reaches

the site boundary when detections are present. Therefore, the data supports the fact that releases were not leaving the site via the surface water pathway. The groundwater standards were restricted to agricultural uses since BLM has control over land uses and no residential supply wells could be installed in the area. This last ARAR refinement (e.g., domestic versus agricultural uses) left only iron and manganese as being released by the landfill. Both of these constituents are not a CERCLA hazardous substance so the site was given a No Further Remedial Action Planned (NFRAP) status by the EPA.

The BLM and EPA worked closely together to develop a site-specific Sampling and Analysis Plan (SAP) and Quality Assurance Project Plan (QAPP). The strategy of the SAP specifically addressed the ephemeral conditions of the site and defined the actual release pathways.

AML	Abandoned Mine Land
ARAR(s)	Applicable or Relevant and Appropriate Requirement(s)
BDAT	Best Demonstrated Available Technology
BLM	Bureau of Land Management
CAA	Clean Air Act
CDPHE	Colorado Department of Public Health and the Environment
CERCLA	Comprehensive Environmental Response, Compensation, and Liability Act
CFR	Code of Federal Regulations
CWA	Clean Water Act
EE/CA	Engineering Evaluation/Cost Analysis
EPA	Environmental Protection Agency
LDR	Land Disposal Restrictions
MCL	Maximum Contaminant Level
NAAQS	National Ambient Air Quality Standards
NCP	National Oil and Hazardous Substances Pollution Contingency Plan, also known as the National Contingency Plan
NFRAP	No Further Remedial Action Planned
NHPA	National Historic Preservation Act
NPDES	National Pollution Elimination Discharge
NPL	National Priorities List
NSPS	New Source Performance Standards
OAR	Oregon Administrative Rules
ODEQ	Oregon Department of Environmental Quality
OSWER	Office of Solid Waste and Emergency Response
RCRA	Resource Conservation and Recovery Act
RI/FS	Remedial Investigation/Feasibility Study
ROD	Record of Decision
R&PP	Recreational and Public Purpose
RSI	Remedial Site Inspection
QAPP	Quality Assurance Project Plan
SAP	Sampling and Analysis Plan
SARA	Superfund Amendments and Reauthorization Act

Abbreviations and Acronyms

SDWA	Safe Drinking Water Act
SIP	State Implementation Plan
SSL	Soil Screening Levels
TBC	To Be Considered
TCLP	Toxicity Characteristic Leaching Procedure
TMDL	Total Maximum Daily Load
TSCA	Toxic Substance Control Act
USC	United States Code
WET	Waste Extraction Test
WQCC	Water Quality Control Commission

Federal ARARs

Table A-1. Summary of Potential Chemical-Specific ARARs

Standard, Requirement, Criteria, or Limitation	Citation	Description/Comments
Clean Water Act (CWA)	33 USC 1251-1387 Chapter 26	The primary purpose of the Clean Water Act, also known as the Federal Water Pollution Control Act, is to restore and maintain the quality of surface waters by restricting discharges of all designated pollutants, which include 126 "priority toxic pollutants," various "conventional pollutants," and certain "non-conventional pollutants."
National Pollutant Discharge Elimination System (NPDES)	CWA 402 40 CFR 122 and 125	Regulates the discharge of treated effluent and storm water runoff to waters of the United States. Potentially applicable substantive NPDES standards include technology-based pollutant controls, or effluent standards, governing surface water discharges.
Safe Drinking Water Act	40 CFR 141-149	Substantive Safe Drinking Water Act requirements that may be applicable or relevant and appropriate at CERCLA sites include: drinking water standards, restrictions on the underground injection of wastes, and groundwater protection programs.
National Primary Drinking Water Standards	40 CFR 141	Establishes health-based standards (maximum contaminant levels or MCLs) for public drinking water systems.
National Secondary Drinking Water Regulations	40 CFR 143	Establishes welfare-based standards for public water systems (secondary MCLs).
Federal Water Quality Criteria	40 CFR 131	Sets standards for surface water to protect aquatic organisms and human health.
Resource Conservation and Recovery Act (RCRA) - Lists of Hazardous Wastes	40 CFR 261, Subpart D	Defines those solid mining-related wastes which are subject to regulation as hazardous wastes under 40 CFR Parts 262-265, and Parts 124, 270, and 271.
RCRA	40 CFR 268	The temporary or permanent placement of restricted hazardous wastes on the land at a CERCLA site may trigger RCRA land disposal restrictions (LDR) treatment standards as applicable requirements. LDR treatment standards, which vary depending on the type of hazardous waste being treated, are concentration- and technology-based standards designed to reduce the mobility and toxicity of hazardous constituents present in hazardous wastes. In order for LDR treatment standards to apply, placement of restricted hazardous wastes must occur.
RCRA	40 CFR 261.4(b)(7) and RCRA Section 3001(b) (Bevill Amendment)	Not all hazardous wastes are necessarily subject to LDR treatment standards. The Bevill Amendment excludes certain solid waste resulting from mining operations, specifically the beneficiation of minerals, from the definition of hazardous wastes and Subtitle C requirements.
Toxic Substance Control Act (TSCA)	15 U.S.C. s/s 2601 et seq. (1976)	Creates a broad range of chemical control measures including information gathering, chemical testing, labeling, inspection, storage, and disposal requirements. Chemicals regulated under the TSCA include asbestos, CFCs used as aerosol propellants, hexavalent chromium, and polychlorinated biphenyls (PCBs). The TSCA governs many aspects of PCB management, including the cleanup of spills, storage, and disposal.

Table A-1. Summary of Potential Chemical-Specific ARARs

Standard, Requirement, Criteria, or Limitation	Citation	Description/Comments
Clean Air Act (CAA)	42 USC 7401	Only Titles I and III of the CAA are likely to directly affect a Superfund remedial action, since on-site CERCLA actions are not subject to administrative procedures and permit requirements (found within Title V of the CAA).
National Ambient Air Quality Standards (NAAQSs)	42 USC 7401	Title I of the CAA requires the EPA to publish NAAQSs, or acceptable environmental levels, for "criteria pollutants." To carry out this mandate, the EPA requires each State to identify areas that have attained NAAQSs for criteria pollutants (classified as "attainment areas") and those that have not (classified as "non-attainment areas"). The EPA also requires each State to submit a State Implementation Plan (SIP) showing how NAAQSs will eventually be achieved in non-attainment areas or will be maintained in attainment areas.
New Source Performance Standards (NSPS)	42 USC 7401	NSPSs, promulgated pursuant to Title I of the CAA, only apply to certain major new sources and major modifications of existing sources that emit "designated pollutants" (which are different than criteria pollutants). The particular source categories governed by the NSPS are generally not found at CERCLA sites, and are therefore not applicable requirements. They may, however, be relevant and appropriate if the pollutants emitted or technologies employed during a response action are sufficiently similar to an NSPS designated pollutant or source category.
National Primary and Secondary Ambient Air Quality Standards	40 CFR 50	Sets standards on ambient concentrations of carbon monoxide, lead, nitrogen dioxide, PM10, ozone, and sulfur oxides.
National Emission Standards for Hazardous Air Pollutants	40 CFR 61	Regulates emission of hazardous chemicals to the atmosphere from stationary sources.

Table A-2. Summary of Potential Location-Specific ARARs

Standard, Requirement, Criteria, or Limitation	Citation	Description/Comments
National Historic Preservation Act (NHPA)	16 USC 470 et seq. A portion of 40 CFR 6.301 (b), 36 CFR 63 and 800	Requires Federal agencies to take into account the effect of any federally assisted undertaking or licensing on any district, site, building, structure, or object that is included in, or eligible for, inclusion in the National Register of Historic Places. Regulates inventory, assessment, and consultation on project effects and protection measures for cultural properties on Federal lands.
Native American Graves Protection and Repatriation Act (NAGPRA)	25 USC 3001-3013 43 CFR Part 10	Regulations that pertain to the identification, protection, and appropriate disposition of human remains, funerary objects, sacred objects, or objects of cultural patrimony.
The Historic and Archaeological Preservation Act of 1974	16 USC 469 40 CFR 6.301(c)	Establishes procedures to provide for preservation of significant scientific, prehistoric, historic, and archeological data, which might be destroyed through alteration of terrain as a result of a Federal construction project or a federally licensed activity or program.
Historic Sites, Buildings, and Antiquities Act	16 USC 461 through 467; 40 CFR 6.301(a)	Requires Federal agencies to consider the existence and location of landmarks on the National Registry of Natural Landmarks to avoid undesirable impacts on such landmarks.
Executive Order 11593	16 USC 461- 467 40 CFR 6.301(a)	Provides for the inventory and nomination of historical and archeological sites.
The Archaeological Resources Protection Act of 1979	43 CFR 7	Regulates requirements for authorized removal of archeological resources from public or tribal lands.
Federal Land Policy and Management Act of 1976 (FLPMA)	43 USC 1701	Provides for multiple use and inventory, protection, and planning for cultural resources on public lands.
Executive Order No. 11990 - Protection of Wetlands	40 CFR 6.302(a) and Appendix A	Requires Federal agencies conducting certain activities to avoid, to the extent possible, the adverse impacts associated with the destruction or loss of wetlands and to avoid support of new construction in wetlands if a practicable alternative exists.
Executive Order No. 11988 - Floodplain Management	40 CFR 6.302(b) and Appendix A	Requires Federal agencies to evaluate the potential effects of actions they may take in a floodplain to avoid, to the extent possible, adverse effects associated with direct and indirect development of a floodplain.
Section 404, Clean Water Act (CWA)	33 CFR 330	Regulates discharge of dredge or fill materials into waters of the United States.

Table A-2. Summary of Potential Location-Specific ARARs

Standard, Requirement, Criteria, or Limitation	Citation	Description/Comments
Fish and Wildlife Coordination Act	40 CFR 6.302(g)	Requires coordination with Federal and State agencies to provide adequate protection of fish and wildlife resources. Specifically, consultation is required when any modification or any stream or other water body is considered as part of the action.
Endangered Species Act (ESA)	16 USC 1531(h) through 1543; 50 CFR 17, 402, and 40 CFR 6.302(b)	Regulates the protection of threatened or endangered species and critical habitat. Requires action to conserve endangered species within critical habitat upon which species depend. Activity may not jeopardize continued existence of endangered species or destroy or adversely modify a critical habitat. Includes consultation with the Department of the Interior.
RCRA	40 CFR 264	Specifies requirements for locating hazardous waste facilities.
Wild and Scenic Rivers Act	16 USC 1271-1287, Public Law 90-542	Establishes a National Wild and Scenic Rivers System for the protection of rivers with important scenic, recreational, fish and wildlife, and other values. Rivers are classified as wild, scenic, or recreational. The Act designates specific rivers for inclusion in the System and prescribes the methods and standards by which additional rivers may be added. The Act contains procedures and limitations for control of lands in federally administered components of the System and for disposition of lands and minerals under Federal ownership.

Table A-3. Summary of Potential Action-Specific ARARs

Standard, Requirement, Criteria, or Limitation	Citation	Description/Comments
Hazardous Materials Transportation Act - Standards Applicable to Transport of Hazardous Materials	49 USC 1801-1813 40 CFR 107, 171-177	Regulates the transportation of hazardous waste.
Criteria for Classification of Solid Waste Disposal Facilities and Practices	40 CFR 257	Establishes criteria for determining which solid waste disposal practices pose a reasonable probability of adverse effects on health or the environment and, thereby, constitute prohibited open dumps.
Criteria for Municipal Solid Waste Landfills	40 CFR 258	Establishes criteria for municipal solid waste landfills.
Standards Applicable to Generation of Hazardous Waste	40 CFR 262	Establishes standards for the generation of hazardous waste. Exempt through 40 CFR 261.4(b)(7)
Standards Applicable to Transporters of Hazardous Waste	40 CFR 263	Regulates the transportation of hazardous waste. Establishes standards which apply to persons transporting hazardous waste within the United States if the transportation requires a manifest under 40 CFR 262.
RCRA Standards for Owners and Operators of Hazardous Waste Treatment, Storage, and Disposal Facilities Design and Operating Requirements	40 CFR 264, pursuant to 42 USC 6924, 6925	Among the potentially applicable substantive RCRA standards are design and operating specifications for hazardous waste treatment, storage, and disposal units used at Superfund sites. For example, RCRA hazardous waste incinerator performance standards (Part 264, Subpart O), such as destruction and removal efficiency and limits on hydrogen chloride and particulate matter emissions, are applicable to hazardous waste incinerators used during remedial actions. RCRA design and operating standards are also applicable to containers and tanks used to store hazardous wastes at CERCLA sites (Part 264, Subparts I and J). RCRA land disposal unit design and operating standards, known collectively as minimum technological requirements, apply when permanent on-site disposal of hazardous wastes in landfills, waste piles, surface impoundments, or land treatment units is part of the remedy (Part 264, Subpart N).
RCRA Groundwater Monitoring	40 CFR 264, Subpart F	Additional RCRA standards may be applicable to hazardous waste land disposal units at CERCLA sites. RCRA groundwater monitoring standards, which involve the use of monitoring wells to detect the presence of contaminants in underlying aquifers, are applicable when a Superfund response involves the creation of a new land disposal unit or the remediation of an existing land disposal unit.

Table A-3. Summary of Potential Action-Specific ARARs

Standard, Requirement, Criteria, or Limitation	Citation	Description/Comments
RCRA Closure and Post-Closure Care	40 CFR 264, Subpart G	RCRA closure and post-closure requirements may also be applicable to on-site hazardous waste management units, such as tanks, waste piles, and surface impoundments, which are taken out of service at Superfund sites. There are two types of potentially applicable RCRA closure schemes: clean closure and landfill closure. Clean closure involves removing or decontaminating all waste residues, contaminated equipment, and contaminated soils so that no additional care or monitoring is required, either at RCRA or CERCLA sites. Landfill closure involves leaving hazardous wastes and contaminated equipment in place, and may trigger applicable requirements, such as the use of a final cap or cover for the unit and continued groundwater monitoring in the post-closure period.
Clean Water Act National Pollutant Discharge Elimination System	33 USC 1342 40 CFR 122	Requires permits for the discharge of pollutants from any point source into waters of the United States.
Federal Mine Safety and Health Act	30 USC 801-962	Regulates worker safety at active mine sites.
Surface Mining Control and Reclamation Act	30 USC 1201- 1326 30 CFR 816 30 CFR 784	Protects the environment from effects of surface coal mining operations.

Table A-4. Summary of Potential Federal Advisories, Criteria, Policy, or Guidance To Be Considered (TBCs)

Standard, Requirement, Criteria, or Limitation	Citation	Description/Comments
BLM Risk Management Criteria	Technical Note 390, Revised 2004	Suggests acceptable multimedia criteria for heavy metals as they relate to recreational use and wildlife habitat on BLM lands.
Interim Guidance on Establishing Soil Lead Cleanup Levels at Superfund Sites	EPA Directive #9355.4-02, September, 1989	Suggests levels for lead in soil. This factor would be considered if lead is found in elevated levels in soils remaining after contaminant removal.
U.S. Environmental Protection Agency Soil Screening Guidance	EPA Document Number: EPA540/R-96/018, July 1996 Supplemental Guidance for Developing Soil Screening Levels for Superfund Sites, Office of Solid Waste and Emergency Response (OSWER) 9355.4-24	The Soil Screening Guidance is a tool developed by the EPA to help standardize and accelerate the evaluation and cleanup of contaminated soils at sites on the National Priorities List (NPL) where future residential land use is anticipated. The Guidance presents a framework for developing risk-based, soil screening levels (SSLs) for protection of human health. The User's Guide provides a simple step-by-step methodology for environmental science/engineering professionals to calculate risk-based, site-specific SSLs for contaminants in soil that may be used to identify areas needing further investigation at NPL sites.
General Procedural Guidance for Native American Consultation	H-8160-1	Before making decisions or approving actions that could result in changes in land use, physical changes to lands or resources, changes in access, or alienation of lands, BLM managers must determine whether Native American interests would be affected, observe pertinent consultation requirements, and document how this was done.

Table A-4. Summary of Potential Federal Advisories, Criteria, Policy, or Guidance To Be Considered (TBCs)

Standard, Requirement, Criteria, or Limitation	Citation	Description/Comments
National Ambient Air Quality Standards (NAAQS)	Title I of Clean Air Act	Requires the EPA to publish NAAQS, or acceptable environmental levels, for "criteria pollutants." To carry out this mandate, the EPA requires each State to identify areas that have attained NAAQS for criteria pollutants (classified as "attainment areas") and those that have not (classified as "non-attainment areas"). The EPA also requires each State to submit a State Implementation Plan (SIP) showing how NAAQS will eventually be achieved in non-attainment areas or will be maintained in attainment areas. Any substantive standards contained within the SIP are, however, federally enforceable, and are potential ARARs.
Wellhead Protection Programs	—	The SDWA wellhead protection program is a State-implemented initiative intended to protect wells and groundwater recharge areas that supply public drinking water systems. Elements of State wellhead protection programs may be ARARs at CERCLA sites.
BLM Response Actions Handbook 1703-1	—	
BLM Abandoned Mine Land (AML) Handbook	—	